THE 10

Most Innovative Bands

Peggy Jo Wilhelm

Series Editor
Jeffrey D. Wilhelm

Much thought, debate, and research went into choosing and ranking the 10 items in each book in this series. We realize that everyone has his or her own opinion of what is most significant, revolutionary, amazing, deadly, and so on. As you read, you may agree with our choices, or you may be surprised — and that's the way it should be!

Franklin Watts

an imprint of

SCHOLASTIC

www.scholastic.com/librarypublishing

A Rubicon book published in association with Scholastic Inc.

Ru'bicon © 2008 Rubicon Publishing Inc.
www.rubiconpublishing.com

Associate Publishers: Kim Koh, Miriam Bardswich
Project Editor: Amy Land
Editor: Christine Boocock
Creative Director: Jennifer Drew
Project Manager/Designer: Jeanette MacLean

The publisher gratefully acknowledges the following for permission to reprint copyrighted material in this book.

Every reasonable effort has been made to trace the owners of copyrighted material and to make due acknowledgment. Any errors or omissions drawn to our attention will be gladly rectified in future editions.

"A Love Supreme" (excerpt) from Joe Maita/Jerry Jazz Musician/ www.jerryjazz.com

"British band Radiohead letting fans set the price for new album" (excerpt) by Cassandra Szklarski, October 1, 2007. Copyright by: The Canadian Press.

Cover image: The Beatles–Photo by Hulton Archive/Getty Images

Library and Archives Canada Cataloguing in Publication

Wilhelm, Peggy Jo
        The 10 most innovative bands / Peggy Jo Wilhelm.

Includes index.
ISBN: 978-1-55448-554-3

        1. Readers (Elementary). 2. Readers--Rock Groups.
I. Title. II. Title: Ten most innovative bands.

PE1117.W538 2007   428.6   C2007-906950-9

1 2 3 4 5 6 7 8 9 10   10   17 16 15 14 13 12 11 10 09 08

Printed in Singapore

Contents

14

18

26

YOU SAY YOU WANT A REVOLU...

When you turn on the radio, what do you usually hear? Do the songs immediately reel you in, or does everything sound exactly the same? It's rare for an artist or band with an original, refreshing sound to come along. When it happens, though, everyone starts listening! Musicians who push boundaries demand listeners' attention. They can even transform musical genres with their sound.

In this book, you'll discover the 10 most innovative bands. These musicians opened our ears and minds to new musical possibilities. Their innovative, groundbreaking sounds changed the face of music worldwide. They have influenced many of the artists you listen to today in one way or another.

In choosing and ranking the bands on our list, we considered these criteria: the extent to which, through its own unique sound, the band changed the direction of music; the level of its influence on other musicians; the critical acclaim and number of fans it has won; and the band's lasting impact and fame in the music industry.

Next time you turn on the radio, listen for bands with a fresh, unique sound. It's these artists that are pushing boundaries and making music that stands out!

---

genres: *types or categories of music*
innovative: *ahead of the times; original*
acclaim: *enthusiastic approval*

TION?

Which band is the most innovative?

10 TWELVE GIRLS

The band's debut album, Beautiful Energy, sold more than two million copies in Japan. It still holds the record for the highest sales of any Chinese artist in that country!

BAND

FORMED: 2001

MUSICAL GENRE: Traditional Chinese, pop, jazz, classical

INSIDE SCOOP: Twelve Girls Band actually consists of 13 musicians! Twelve is a symbolic number in China, so the band's producer kept it in the band's name. Only 12 members of the group perform at the same time.

It might sound unusual, but sometimes people look to the past to create something innovative in the present. Twelve Girls Band is a modern creation. But this group is based on ancient female orchestras. Called *Yue Fang*, these groups played in the courts of the Chinese Tang dynasty — between A.D. 618 and 906! In 2001, producer Wang Xiaojing (shiow-jing) decided to bring back this ancient form of entertainment. He hired classically trained female Chinese musicians. He had them play a mix of modern and traditional music. The result? The highly successful Twelve Girls Band!

Twelve Girls Band is the first internationally successful female band from China. Wang chose members of the band from China's leading music schools. He hired women who were skilled at playing more than one traditional Chinese instrument. Playing a mix of modern and classical tunes, the band first became famous in China and Japan. Soon, their concerts in North America were selling out as well.

"Nobody has ever experienced this form of concert in the past." This is what band member Ma Jingjing told a reporter in a 2005 interview. And she was right! The band has mixed traditional Chinese music with modern Western tunes in a truly innovative way.

TWELVE GIRLS BAND

MUSIC MAKERS

Twelve Girls Band is a 13-member group of women playing ancient Chinese instruments. The band's traditional instruments give the group its unique sound. Among the band's instruments are the *pipa*, the *erhu*, and the *dizi*. The *pipa* is a plucked instrument. It looks like a pear-shaped guitar with four strings. The *erhu* is like a two-stringed violin. The *dizi* is a flute made out of bamboo. All 13 members of the group trained at China's most famous music schools.

? Do you think Twelve Girls Band might be starting a trend? In what ways are the structure of the band and the group's music unique?

Quick Fact

In 2004, *Eastern Energy*, the band's first album to be released in the U.S., entered the Billboard chart at #62. This marked the highest debut in Billboard history by an Asian band!

SINGULAR SOUND

Not many bands on the radio are rockin' out on the *dizi* or the *pipa*! Twelve Girls Band's instruments set it apart. The band has introduced North American audiences to new sounds through its music. "I think our popularity is due to the way we present our music," says band member Tina Sun. "Our manager's vision was to take classical music and meld it together with modern music."

? Twelve Girls Band plays traditional instruments that are unfamiliar to many people. Are you surprised that they have such a huge following? Explain why or why not.

ONE OF A KIND!

Twelve Girls Band is "China's first all-women traditional instrument ensemble," according to the *China Daily*. The band has an unusual repertoire that also helps it stand out. As written in the *China Daily*, "Mixing exquisite Chinese classical music with the rhythm of jazz, rock and roll, and hip hop, [Twelve Girls Band's] unique performance is a real eye-opener." Apart from the music, the band also pays attention to "stage design, visual effects, clothing, and mode of performance," says producer Wang Xiaojing. By doing this, the group hopes to "create entirely new folk music that is pleasant both to the ear and to the eye."

meld: *merge; blend*
ensemble: *group of musicians*
repertoire: *list of pieces performed*
exquisite: *extraordinarily beautiful*

? How important is image to a band's career? Do you think that focusing on image can help a band get its music noticed? Explain.

Recipe for Success!

This checklist will show you the ingredients that went into creating Twelve Girls Band. All these ingredients existed before the band. However, when combined, they resulted in an innovative approach to modern music.

1 bunch of Cantopop style

Cantopop is short for "Cantonese popular music." It combines a soft, American rock style with traditional Chinese singing. Though the members of Twelve Girls Band don't sing, they do copy the type of squeaky-clean image of Cantopop stars. "Perky, dreamy, neatly dressed, well behaved, they are the rock stars any mom would want her kid to marry," according to *TIME* magazine writer Richard Corliss.

Lots of Sizhu

Sizhu is the name for certain Chinese chamber music ensembles made up of string and wind instruments. The term also refers to the type of music they play. These ensembles play a form of instrumental music from southern China. The *dizi* and *erhu* are common *Sizhu* instruments.

The Expert Says...

"There's something mesmerizing about the band's graceful stage presence, their technical virtuosity — and most of all, their euphoric expressions as they play their instruments."

— Ilya Garger, *TIME* magazine

virtuosity: *technical skill*
euphoric: *overjoyed*

Dash of Western pop music

Twelve Girls Band plays a little of everything. The band covers famous jazz tunes. It has also recorded unique versions of songs by some of the music world's hottest recording artists! In 2005, the band even released an album called *Twelve Girls of Christmas* filled with interesting versions of festive favorites.

Take Note

Twelve Girls Band takes the #10 spot. This group defines unique! It is unlike any other popular band out there. Twelve Girls Band has brought a Chinese sound to Western audiences. The group has popularized a new style of music. The band has also gained millions of fans and won awards along the way.
- Twelve Girls Band was created by a music producer who had a great money-making idea. Does this affect how you feel about the band? Does the fact that this group was put together and didn't form on its own, make it any less impressive? Explain.

5   4   3   2   1

Digable Planets in 1994

NETS

FORMED: 1991

MUSICAL GENRE: Alternative rap, hip hop, jazz

INSIDE SCOOP: Why is each member of this jazz-flavored rap trio named after an insect? As Ladybug, aka Mary Ann Vieira, explains, "Insects stick together and work for mutually beneficial causes."

Rap music might seem old school now, but it has only really been popular for 28 years! In 1979, a group called the Sugarhill Gang released an album called *Rapper's Delight*. With this release, rap music was thrust into the spotlight. A lot of people thought rap was just a fad. But as the genre evolved, it became clear that rap was here to stay.

In less than three decades, rap has developed many different branches, or sub-categories. A genre called jazz-rap is where Digable Planets come in. Jazz emphasizes a swing beat, improvisation, and a relaxed vibe. The group made its mark in 1993, with the release of *Reachin' (A New Refutation of Time and Space)*. "[They] epitomized the laid-back charm of jazz hipsters better than any group before or since," according to music writer John Bush.

Digable Planets helped define a genre. The group expertly combined rap with funky jazz beats. Its inspiration was part Sugarhill Gang and part jazz greats like Miles Davis and Charlie Parker. The group's fame helped increase rap's popularity. Suddenly, rap was known as much for the smooth, mellow feel of a Digable Planets tune as for the aggressive sound of gangsta rap.

---

improvisation: *composing, performing, or delivering without previous preparation*
epitomized: *were a typical example of*

DIGABLE PLANETS

MUSIC MAKERS

Mary Ann Vieira first met Ishmael Butler and Craig Irving in college. The three discovered that they shared a similar interest in music. Soon, Digable Planets was born! Vieira chose "Ladybug" as her nickname. Butler went with "Butterfly," and Irving chose "Doodlebug." The group came to be known as "a communal clan of poet-rappers that made 'hip-hop bebop' popular," according to Ladybug's official Web site. The group was only together for two years before its debut album shot it to fame.

bebop: *type of jazz*

Billboard magazine writer Larry Flick once wrote that, "Ladybug makes great strides in proving women in rap don't need to scream and swagger in order to be tough and assertive." Research some of today's famous female rappers. Are they following Ladybug's lead? Explain.

swagger: *show off*

Mary Ann "Ladybug Mecca" Vieira

Quick Fact

In 1993, Digable Planets won a Grammy Award for "Rebirth of Slick (Cool like Dat)." In 2007, the song was featured on the soundtrack for the movie *Freedom Writers*.

SINGULAR SOUND

Digable Planets was "one of the bands that [was] instrumental in bridging jazz and hip hop," according to writer Oliver Wang. The group also made sure to write meaningful lyrics. Digable Planets' debut album was "a breath of fresh air in a genre dominated by gangsta rap and dance-floor anthems," according to writer Jim Harrington. "[The album] made professing hope, positive speaking, and respecting women seem [cool]." The album also helped launch what some called "alternative rap," according to *Washington Post* writer Richard Harrington.

ONE OF A KIND!

This group's innovative sound helped redefine rap and hip hop. "Rebirth of Slick (Cool Like Dat)," the band's famous single, "was a triumph of cool jazz, hot beats, and laid-back bohemian attitude," according to writer Tina Maples. The three members of the group went their separate ways in 1995. However, with an album that was named "one of the most successful hip-hop records ever made" by music writer Jack Isles, the group definitely made its mark.

instrumental: *responsible*
bohemian: *unconventional in appearance and behavior*

Digable Planets used their lyrics to promote social consciousness and justice. What music do you listen to that addresses social or political issues? How does the music help support the message?

The Expert Says...

" They're groovy bohemian black people, and they're very good at using language. … They bring all their experiences into making something new. "

— Scott Poulson-Bryant, *Vibe* magazine

JAZZY JUNCTION!

DIGABLE PLANETS BECAME FAMOUS FOR BRINGING A JAZZ FLAVOR TO HIP HOP. GET TO KNOW SOME OF THE ARTISTS THAT HELPED DIGABLE PLANETS DEFINE THEIR SOUND IN THIS LIST.

Craig "Doodlebug" Irving

Art Blakey

Born in 1919, Blakey was one of the most important drummers and band leaders in jazz history. During his career, Blakey became famous for playing hard bop jazz. This fiery genre is the flip side to the cool, relaxed sounds of West Coast jazz. Digable Planets used prerecorded Art Blakey music on their hit single "Rebirth of Slick (Cool Like Dat)."

Sonny Rollins

Rollins is "one of the all-time great tenor saxophonists," according to music critic Scott Yanow. He played bebop — a form of modern jazz distinguished by a fast tempo and improvisation. On the single "Time and Space (a New Refutation of)," Digable Planets rap over a sample of a Sonny Rollins tune.

Curtis Mayfield

Mayfield was a singer and songwriter. Most of his work falls under the genres of jazz, funk, and soul. Mayfield "[spoke] about African-American pride and community struggle in his compositions," according to writer Richie Unterberger. Mayfield's music and message inspired the Digable Planets. The band used a Curtis Mayfield sample on a song from their album *Reachin' (A New Refutation of Time and Space)*.

Ishmael "Butterfly" Butler

Quick Fact

The title of the trio's Grammy-winning tune, "Rebirth of Slick (Cool Like Dat)," refers to a famous jazz album by Miles Davis from 1950 called *Birth of the Cool*.

---

sample: *short selection from an old song used as part of a new song*
funk: *rhythm-based music performed with electronic guitars, basses, and organs, as well as saxophones and other wind instruments*

Take Note

Digable Planets secure the #9 spot. The group meshed jazz with rap's urban vibe. It took rap in a different direction with its intelligent, politically-charged lyrics and refusal to follow the crowd. This helped the genre appeal to a wider audience. Despite its fame, the group split in 1995.
• This group broke up at the height of its fame. Give some reasons why a successful band might break up after reaching its goals.

5   4   3   2   1

8 NICKEL CREEK

Band members Chris Thile, Sara Watkins, and Sean Watkins perform in 2007.

FORMED: 1989

MUSICAL GENRE: Progressive bluegrass, country, folk pop

INSIDE SCOOP: When sibling duo Sean and Sara Watkins joined forces with musician Chris Thile, the band they formed became a word-of-mouth sensation!

This trio definitely isn't following the crowd. The music it plays — a mix of bluegrass, rock, jazz, and country — is completely unique. It's so distinctive that it has even caused controversy among traditional bluegrass fans! They've accused Nickel Creek of tampering with tradition. And how do these musicians respond? According to guitarist Sean Watkins, "[We] just don't worry about categorizing it at all — we just try to make the best music we can." For Nickel Creek, bluegrass is just part of a recipe for success.

Bluegrass is a form of American folk music, which emerged in the 1940s. Traditional bluegrass is acoustic music played with banjos, mandolins, guitars, and fiddles. Bluegrass music is fast and lively. It has folk, Celtic, and blues influences.

It's no wonder people label Nickel Creek a bluegrass band. The three members met at bluegrass concerts. As kids, each trained in traditional bluegrass music. In 2000, the group even won the International Bluegrass Music Association award for emerging artist of the year! Despite all this, Nickel Creek has pushed the boundaries of the genre. The group's original songs and ability to blend genres have helped it stand out. This innovative approach is helping Nickel Creek create progressive bluegrass music.

American folk music: *broad category of music that has formed the basis for many other genres; traditional American music*
mandolins: *small, pear-shaped, string instruments*
Celtic: *relating to Scotland, Ireland, or Wales*
progressive: *modern; revolutionary*

NICKEL CREEK

MUSIC MAKERS

Amazingly, these three young musicians have been playing together for over 18 years! All three were preteens when their band was formed. Starting at such a young age, these three were able to develop a unique sound together. They named their band after a bluegrass song written by fiddler Byron Berline. "At the time, we were a much more traditional-sounding bluegrass band," says Sean Watkins. "Nickel Creek sounded like the right kind of name." As the musicians matured and became more courageous, they experimented with every kind of music — from rock and pop to jazz!

Nickel Creek band members from left to right: violinist Sara Watkins, mandolinist Chris Thile, and guitarist Sean Watkins

Quick Fact

The group's album *This Side* won the 2002 Grammy Award for Best Contemporary Folk Album.

SINGULAR SOUND

In the beginning, Nickel Creek "refused to be pigeonholed, mixing and matching genres without staying true to any," according to writer Michael McCall. The band's fast playing, traditional instruments, and energetic songs show its bluegrass roots. But Nickel Creek focuses on taking bluegrass into new territory. The members of the band write much of their own material. They write about modern topics that traditional bluegrass artists don't usually explore. The group's songs are unique because they blend genres. The band's all-acoustic sound is also unusual in our electronic age.

pigeonholed: *placed in a specific category*

ONE OF A KIND!

Nickel Creek blends musical styles in an appealing way. Its success has helped bring progressive bluegrass (also known as newgrass) music to an international audience. Throughout their careers, the band members have performed "spirited live sets that have altered the fabric of what acoustic music can be," according to *Rolling Stone* writer Andrew Dansby. From the time it was formed, this band has focused on exploring new musical styles. The band has challenged what people think of as bluegrass music. One of few famous bands playing progressive bluegrass, Nickel Creek has helped reinvent this genre for the 21st century.

Quick Fact

Among the band's more unusual covers are its versions of Radiohead's "Nice Dream" and Britney Spears's "Toxic"!

? The members of Nickel Creek describe being in a band and performing as a type of education. What do you think they mean by this? How do you think musicians keep growing and learning?

? Imagine "Toxic" played on the fiddle! In what ways do you think Nickel Creek's versions of popular songs sound different than the originals?

10   9   **8**   7   6

In Praise of
MODERN MELODIES!

Some of the most important newspapers and magazines have praised Nickel Creek's innovative music. Read what has been written about the band in these quotes.

"... Arguably the finest acoustic string ensemble operating today. ... Nickel Creek is the future of American acoustic music, and the future never looked rosier."
— *Chicago Tribune*

"The trio is making down-home music relevant for a new generation. ... To hear Nickel Creek is to hear the vibrant reinvention of a classic form."
— *TIME* magazine

"... Nickel Creek blends bluegrass, classical music, and pop with irresistible aplomb, and sings like angels to boot."
— *Washington Post*

"[Nickel Creek is] the single most original and inventive bluegrass band to emerge in the early '00s."
— *Charles Spano, allmusic.com*

aplomb: *self-confidence; style*

Since forming Nickel Creek, Sean Watkins (far right) has released three solo albums. His sister, Sara, has plans to record her first solo album. Chris Thile has also kept busy over the years with five solo albums!

The Expert Says...

"Each new album further underline[s] the group's unwillingness to sit around and rehash all-too-familiar bluegrass formulas."

— Jason Killingsworth, *Paste* magazine

rehash: *use again with no significant changes*

Take Note

Nickel Creek runs away with the #8 spot. This award-winning group has been around for almost two decades. All along, the band has refused to conform to a certain kind of music. Nickel Creek is unique in its style of delivery and in its songwriting. The band's appealing recordings have helped bring progressive bluegrass music to a wide audience of listeners.

• In 2005, Chris Thile told an interviewer, "If we're going to blend genres, we'd like it to be genre soup, where you can't see what's in it — as opposed to genre stew, where everything is very defined." What exactly do you think he meant by this?

5   4   3   2   1

Red Hot Chili Peppers includes (left to right) bassist Michael "Flea" Balzary, vocalist Anthony Kiedis, guitarist John Frusciante, and drummer Chad Smith.

PEPPERS

FORMED: 1983

MUSICAL GENRE: "Indie" funk-rock

INSIDE SCOOP: This band was formed when friends Michael Balzary, aka Flea, and Hillel Slovak convinced Anthony Kiedis to sing in their band instead of becoming a poet and actor.

When a Red Hot Chili Peppers song is on the radio, you can't help but notice! With its unique brand of punk rock, this band is in a class all its own. Despite its current fame, this one-time indie band took a while to catch on. Originally, the band was known as Tony Flow & the Miraculously Majestic Masters of Mayhem. And from day one the band has been about experimentation. The band meshed musical styles and also created a distinct style of live performance. At first, not everyone was sure that the band's innovative sound would sell. In general, established recording companies like a sure thing. They invest in musicians who play music that fans are accustomed to. However, it was this band's quirky style that got it noticed. In 1983, after the band changed its name to the Red Hot Chili Peppers, EMI Records gave the band its first big break.

The Chili Peppers popularized a completely innovative sound. According to music writer Greg Prato, the group created an "intoxicating new musical style by combining funk and punk rock together."

indie: *not represented by a major recording company; independent*

RED HOT CHILI PEPPERS

MUSIC MAKERS

Joined by drummer Jack Irons, Kiedis, Balzary, and Slovak formed a band in the early 1980s. But the road to the top wasn't easy. First, Irons and Slovak left the group. Then the band's debut album, *The Red Hot Chili Peppers*, got disappointing reviews. "The absence of the two original members showed," according to writer Greg Prato. As the band matured, its sound improved. "During the '80s, the Red Hot Chili Peppers were one of America's most popular cult bands," says writer Michael Sutton. As the group's fan base grew, its albums started to catch the attention of important music critics. *Stadium Arcadium*, released in 2006, debuted at #1 on the SoundScan album chart!

cult: *attractive to a small, specific group*

The Red Hot Chili Peppers are famous for mixing punk rock, funk, rap, and blues into a new style of music. Name some other bands that combine musical genres to create something new. How does this help the evolution of music?

SINGULAR SOUND

As the Red Hot Chili Peppers rose to fame, they were "acknowledged as innovators, one of the first white acts to mix funk and rap with heavy metal," according to *Rolling Stone* writer Alec Foege. You've heard rock, pop, and rap music. You've also probably heard the blues and funk. But have you heard them all together? The Chili Peppers' signature sound is a combination of all of these styles. The band's song lyrics explore a number of serious political and social issues. Yet these lyrics also stay true to the group's spirit of zany playfulness.

Quick Fact

Funk music legend George Clinton produced the Chili Peppers' 1985 album *Freaky Styley*. He helped the band capture a "pure funk sound," says writer Jason Birchmeier.

ONE OF A KIND!

When they were starting out, the Chili Peppers became known for their crazy concert antics. Highly energetic, rowdy live shows cemented their radical punk reputation. The band's sound also greatly influenced the American music scene. When the Chili Peppers debuted, "Kiedis's broad, surfer-dude rapping was a novel sound," wrote Jody Rosen on slate.com. According to writer Greg Prato, "The Chili Peppers spawned a slew of imitators in their wake." However, as Prato points out, the band "still managed to be the leaders of the pack by the dawn of the 21st century."

antics: *wildly playful or funny actions*
slew: *large number*

Quick Fact

The Red Hot Chili Peppers have really made their mark. The group has won seven Grammy awards and has had 11 #1 singles on the Billboard Modern Rock Chart!

Do you think indie bands have to alter their style when they sign with big labels? Explain.

7

MUSICAL MISHMASH

THE RED HOT CHILI PEPPERS MADE IT BIG BY NOT LIMITING THEMSELVES TO ONE GENRE. FIND OUT MORE ABOUT THE BAND'S APPROACH TO MUSIC IN THIS ARTICLE.

It seems that for the Chili Peppers, making popular music is all about experimentation! According to bassist and founding member Flea, the band doesn't "talk much about songs or how songs should be constructed." The band members simply "start to play and see what happens, how they develop." This method has allowed the group to mesh individual genres into eclectic-sounding songs.

Since each member of the band has been influenced by different musical genres, each one also brings something unique to songwriting. Flea's first love was jazz. Lead singer Anthony Kiedis is a rocker at heart. The songs these musicians create together are in a category all their own. And the band doesn't stop at test-driving new styles. A variety of instruments have also made their way onto the band's nine albums. As Flea told the BBC in 2002, "I've actually played trumpet on a few Chili's albums." He's even tried out the flugelhorn!

In the end, though, it's all about creating something real. As Kiedis told an interviewer in 1994, "We're only really capable of doing something that is directly based on what we feel and what we know and the experiences that we've had."

flugelhorn: *trumpet-like instrument invented in the 18th century*

The Expert Says...

"Few rock groups of the '80s broke down as many musical barriers and were as original as the Red Hot Chili Peppers.

— Greg Prato, allmusic.com

Take Note

The Red Hot Chili Peppers rock into the #7 spot. Soon after its debut, this band took on a cult following. Incredible live performances helped the band gradually increase its fan base. The band's fusion of musical styles and edgy lyrics established the members of the Red Hot Chili Peppers as truly innovative musicians.
• To what degree do sound, look, performance style, and genre help a band achieve success? Which elements do you think are most important? Explain.

RED HOT CHILI PEPPERS

5   4   3   2   1

6 KODO

How does waking up at dawn, going for a six-mile run, then spending the rest of your day doing drills and practicing, sound to you? This is just part of the strict regime that keeps Kodo drummers in tip-top shape!

KODO—© TOBY MELVILLE/REUTERS/CORBIS

West

FORMED: 1981

MUSICAL GENRE: Japanese drumming

INSIDE SCOOP: According to the group, Kodo has two meanings. It means "heartbeat" and can also mean "children of the drum."

Go to one of Kodo's concerts and you know you're not in rock and roll territory anymore! Instead of a full band, there are drums accompanied by flutes, bells, and human voices. Instead of familiar rock tunes, there are traditional pieces that make the drummers the stars. Instead of glitzy costumes, there are traditional Japanese outfits. Some performers even wear *fundoshi* — traditional Japanese underwear!

Kodo's innovative concerts are just one of the draws. This group is famous for its modern take on Japanese *taiko* drumming. Historically, these drums were used on battlefields to coordinate troop movements and scare approaching enemies. They were also used in religious ceremonies and to send messages between towns. Today, *taiko* drums are valued purely as musical instruments.

Kodo drummers perform on a variety of drums. They combine a drum beat with the sound of ancient and modern instruments. In one concert, musicians playing Caribbean steel drums were accompanied by a Japanese harpist! Kodo's sound is modern and innovative. This group has reinvented a traditional art form for modern audiences.

KODO

MUSIC MAKERS

Originally, there were only seven members of Kodo. Today, 23 musicians are part of the group. At the moment, there are 16 male and seven female performers. These musicians live together on Sado Island, Japan. The musicians practice their instruments daily. Because their shows are so physically demanding, they also spend a lot of time exercising. As Michael Church wrote in the *Independent* in 2004, "Unlike Western drummers, who operate from the wrist, these [performers drum] with their whole bodies."

? It's unusual for members of a group to all live together. In what ways do you think this affects Kodo's music? How does it make Kodo different from other musical acts?

SINGULAR SOUND

According to group staff member Yoshiako Oi, Kodo "[does] not perform authentically traditional Japanese music." The group performs on traditional instruments, but often plays modern compositions. With Kodo, "every stroke on every drum and every vocal or handclap ... is carefully planned out and executed crisply," according to writer Adam Greenburg. And it's not all about drums — many other instruments are also part of Kodo's sound. The *fue* and *shamisen* are two instruments featured in the group's songs. The *fue* is a type of Japanese flute. The *shamisen* is a three-stringed instrument played with a pick.

? Kodo plays instruments built according to age-old traditions. Many of the buildings in the group's village on Sado Island were built using reclaimed wood from 200-year-old farmhouses! What does this suggest about the life philosophy of the members of this group?

ONE OF A KIND!

Kodo performs pieces based on traditional Japanese music. But the band also plays pieces composed by modern musicians. A Kodo show is a "unique synthesis of sound, theater, and choreography," according to writer Vivienne Heller of the *Independent*. Audiences feel the drum's vibrations throughout their bodies. They see the athleticism of the powerful drummers. Most importantly, they experience an entirely different type of music firsthand.

---

synthesis: *combination; blend*

? How can musicians reinvent traditions for contemporary audiences? Is there any danger in toying with traditions? Explain.

Quick Fact

Kodo's drummers play some of the largest drums in the world. The *O-daiko* is a drum made from the trunk of an African Bubinga tree. The skin is made from the hide of one cow. This drum measures over three feet across and, together with its stand, weighs over 880 pounds!

8   7   6

GOOD VIBRATIONS

LEARN MORE ABOUT THE ANCIENT ART OF *TAIKO* DRUMMING IN THIS ARTICLE.

Long before telephones and computers became common household items, people relied on other devices to help them communicate. In ancient Japan, drums were used for this purpose. Many historians think that *taiko* drumming has been around for thousands of years. These huge drums, which make deeper, louder sounds than smaller drums, were used to communicate vital messages across long distances. In ancient Japan, community borders were defined by the farthest distance at which the *taiko* could be heard!

Kodo's gigantic drums produce huge, booming sounds. This is the "heartbeat" their name signifies. In 1990, a reviewer wrote that at one Kodo show, "[t]he enormous power of the sound rebounded from the audience and the marble walls, filling the vast space with one huge reverberating heartbeat."

In Kodo's music, the sound of the bigger drums is mixed with the sound produced by a variety of smaller drums. By using many drums, Kodo creates layers of sound. Add this to the group's other instruments and you have a rhythmic, riotous symphony. Audience members say you can feel the music vibrating inside your body!

rebounded: *bounced off of*
reverberating: *echoing*

The Expert Says...

" Kodo is about the drums, the percussion, hearing, and more importantly feeling, the sound through the whole body. "

— Zoe C., music reviewer

percussion: *beating or striking of a musical instrument*

Take Note

Kodo booms into the #6 spot. Drumming has been used for centuries to communicate on the battlefield and between towns, and in religious ceremonies. Kodo has reinvigorated this ancient custom for modern audiences. It has popularized an ancient sound with its creative, groundbreaking music.

- Through its music, Kodo has helped to increase awareness of Japanese culture. Name other bands or musicians that represent a specific culture with their music. Why is it important for a band to bring its culture's traditions to the world?

5   4   3   2   1

Paul Simon (front, with guitar) performs with members of Ladysmith Black Mambazo in 2007.

LADYSMITH BLACK MAMBAZO—© JASON REED/REUTERS/CORBIS

ACK MAMBAZO

FORMED: 1974

MUSICAL GENRE: South African pop

INSIDE SCOOP: This group shot to fame after being discovered by famous musician Paul Simon.

With a name like Ladysmith Black Mambazo, it's no wonder this group has attracted worldwide attention! But it's not just the group's unusual name that has people interested. This  group is famous for its heartfelt, powerful songs.

Lead singer and founder Joseph Shabalala has said that the inspiration for this group came to him in a dream. He wanted to put together a group where voices were the main instruments. Luckily, he didn't have to look much further than his own family to find the performers! The group originally included two of Shabalala's brothers, a few cousins, and a couple of close friends. The men used only their voices to create their music.

A cappella music is popular in South Africa. What set Ladysmith Black Mambazo apart was that the group sang in Zulu. Most South African a cappella groups sang in English or Afrikaans — languages introduced to South Africa by colonial rulers. Singing in Zulu made this group hugely popular with South Africa's native black population. It quickly became the best-selling music group in South Africa!

Ladysmith Black Mambazo's a cappella style is rare in the music world. The group has given "pop a little kick with Zulu melodies," according to *New York Times* writer Jon Pareles. This group has done something totally unique for world music.

a cappella: *music sung without instruments*

LADYSMITH BLACK MAMBAZO

MUSIC MAKERS

The members of this group are known for their impressive harmonies — a mix of tenor, alto, and bass voices. When starting out, this group made a name for itself winning local music competitions. The group was so good that it was eventually banned from competition. People felt this was the only way to give other performers a chance! After appearing on a radio show in 1970, the group got its first recording contract. In 1986, the group appeared on *Graceland* — an album by Paul Simon.

tenor: *highest natural adult male voice*
alto: *lowest female voice; second-highest of the four parts of a chorus*
bass: *lowest pitch or vocal range*

When Paul Simon used Ladysmith Black Mambazo on *Graceland*, some people said he was exploiting African musicians only to promote his own career. Do you think there are both fair and unfair ways for musicians to borrow music from other cultures? Explain.

exploiting: *using selfishly for one's own benefit*

SINGULAR SOUND

"Taking the choral music he heard in the Christian church, [Shabalala] combined it with the Zulu tradition to create his own style," writes music reviewer J. Poet. The group's Zulu sound — high-pitched ululations, noises made in the back of the throat, and tight harmonies — really set it apart. According to Shabalala, before the group came together, "You didn't hear these three sounds in the same songs." It was "new to combine them." The members of the group also use their bodies to make music. Rhythm is marked by foot stomps and hand clapping.

ONE OF A KIND!

Ladysmith Black Mambazo is the world's best-selling group of a style called *isicathamiya* (isi-cot-a-me-ya). This is a traditional Zulu style of a cappella music. It emphasizes vocal harmony and body movements. It was group founder Joseph Shabalala's conversion to Christianity that originally defined the group's music. Despite the religious link, the group's sound "evokes enthusiasm and excitement, regardless of what you follow spiritually," according to Shabalala.

choral: *sung by a choir*
ululations: *long, wobbling cries*

Joseph Shabalala is concerned traditional South African music will die out because of the impact of Western pop music on young generations. How might pop wipe out traditional music?

Quick Fact

Ladysmith Black Mambazo has performed in some pretty impressive places! The group played at two Nobel Peace Prize ceremonies, sang at the 1996 Summer Olympics, and entertained the Queen of England at a 2002 celebration to mark her 50th year on the throne!

Quick Fact

"Ladysmith" is the Shabalala family's hometown in South Africa. "Black" refers to black oxen, the strongest animal on the farm. The Zulu word "Mambazo" means ax. This symbolizes the group's ability to chop down the competition!

10   9   8   7   6

RAISE YOUR VOICE!

A cappella has a long history on the world music scene.
Learn about some of history's most famous voice-only genres in this chart.

MUSIC	ORIGINS	LONGEVITY
Gregorian Chants	Gregorian chants originated as part of European religious ceremonies around the 9th century. Generally sung in Latin and by men, this music is characterized by a single, unaccompanied tune. Singers also hold single syllables across several notes.	In 1994, an album called *Chant* was released by a group of Spanish monks. *Chant* sold more than three million copies in the U.S. alone!
Barbershop	Originally an African-American style of singing, barbershop actually started as a form of entertainment in barber shops. Traditionally, this style calls for four men to sing popular songs in harmony.	Barbershop quartets have kept this 20th-century genre alive and well! Barbershop is a popular style in college and school choirs. There are also dozens of barbershop associations around the world. These help to generate interest in the genre through competitions and concerts.
Doo-wop	Doo-wop first became popular around the 1950s. In this genre, a lead singer is supported by a small group of singers repeating syllables and words as backup.	Doo-wop was originally made famous by groups such as the Platters and the Drifters. After the 1960s the genre's popularity faded.

Quick Fact

In 1987, Ladysmith Black Mambazo won a Grammy Award for Best Traditional Folk Recording. The group won again in 2004 — this time for Best Traditional World Music Album.

The Expert Says...

"When we first started, people did not think it was possible to make money playing *isicathamiya* music."

— Joseph Shabalala, founder and lead singer of Ladysmith Black Mambazo

Take Note

Ladysmith Black Mambazo ranks #5. Just like Kodo and Twelve Girls Band, this group has brought a traditional form of music to an international audience. This group's success has increased interest in a cappella singing. It has also increased awareness of *isicathamiya* music. This group is internationally famous, has won important music awards, and continues to perform at important international events.
- Joseph Shabalala once said, "If my students do not succeed I always criticize myself. ... It is up to me to see they learn correctly." Do you agree with Shabalala's point of view? Explain.

5   4   3   2   1

John Coltrane (center) with the three other members of his quartet, drummer Elvin Jones (left), pianist McCoy Tyner, and bassist Jimmy Garrison.

COLTRANE QUARTET

FORMED: 1962

MUSICAL GENRE: Jazz

INSIDE SCOOP: By the time he formed his own quartet, John Coltrane had already made a name for himself as one of the leading jazz saxophonists of his time.

In 1960, John Coltrane finally stepped into the spotlight. For years, he had played saxophone in other people's bands. He had made a name for himself as a first-rate player. But when Coltrane decided he was ready to form his own group, the jazz world was turned upside down!

Coltrane and his quartet performed together in the 1960s. Together, they transformed the sound of jazz. The music they played was unlike anything people had ever heard before. "At the time … [Coltrane's] playing seemed shockingly radical," writes Nathan Brackett in *The New Rolling Stone Album Guide*. "[H]e was called 'the most avant-garde of the avant-garde.'" Bringing together a pianist, a bass player, and a drummer, Coltrane formed what became known as the Classic John Coltrane Quartet. The band only existed for a few years. However, its impact was huge. Together, these four musicians turned jazz into a more emotional, energetic genre.

The Coltrane Quartet usually played without sheet music. The four musicians were experts at improvisation. According to Brackett, "Parts of Coltrane's early-'60s records now seem like fairly normal jazz." This should come as no surprise seeing as Coltrane and his quartet helped mold jazz into what it is today! According to Brackett, "If anything he did is a cliché, it's because everyone after 'Trane has copped his ideas."

---

avant-garde: *radical; daring; new*
cliché: *overused expression or idea*
copped: *stolen; taken*

THE CLASSIC JOHN COLTRANE QUARTET

MUSIC MAKERS

John Coltrane started playing saxophone as a teenager. In 1945, he joined the navy. A year later, he made his first recording in a quartet with other sailors. After the navy, Coltrane pursued a career as a musician. He played with famous jazz icons such as Dizzy Gillespie and Miles Davis! In 1960, Coltrane left the Davis band. Two years later, he formed the Classic John Coltrane Quartet. Coltrane was accompanied by pianist McCoy Tyner. Jimmy Garrison played bass. Drummer Elvin Jones was the group's fourth member. Together, these musicians altered the jazz genre forever!

? In the 1960s, a lot of people thought this group's music was too "out there." One reviewer of the time even called it "musical nonsense"! In response, Coltrane told a journalist that "music shouldn't be easy to understand." Do you agree or disagree with this statement and why?

Quick Fact
The group's most famous album is *A Love Supreme*. In 2006, the album was named one of *TIME* magazine's 100 Best Albums of All Time. It also came in at #47 on *Rolling Stone* magazine's list of the 500 Greatest Albums of All Time.

SINGULAR SOUND

The Classic John Coltrane Quartet created music that was experimental, innovative, and different. The band's unique style meant that people either loved them or hated them! The group didn't play the bebop style of jazz that was popular during the 1940s. Bebop was all about fast playing. Musicians playing bebop often improvised. But they did so in harmony with the main tune being played. The Classic John Coltrane Quartet became famous for playing modal jazz. Modal jazz had a simpler, more open sound. It wasn't always as harmonious as bebop.

? This group was known for the fiery, complicated music it played at live shows. Several of the group's albums, however, have been called calm and predictable. Give reasons why the quartet might have toned things down on its albums.

ONE OF A KIND!

The Classic John Coltrane Quartet created some of jazz music's most popular and most innovative music. Live, this group was known for each member's lengthy improvisations. Their pounding drums and loud bass were innovative for this time period. The real creative force behind the group was John Coltrane himself. He put the quartet together. He inspired most of the group's music. "Coltrane was a very restless musician who was determined to forge ahead," according to writer Alex Henderson. "[His] quartet did exactly that."

harmonious: *tuneful; melodious; musically pleasing*

? When asked why he created music, Coltrane once replied, "I think music can make the world better, and, if I'm qualified, I want to do it." In what ways can music make the world better? Explain.

Quick Fact
In 2007, John Coltrane was honored by the Pulitzer Prize board. Coltrane was honored posthumously for his amazing talent and for his overall impact on jazz music.

posthumously: *occurring after death*

A LOVE SUPREME

Learn more about the quartet's most famous album in this *Jerry Jazz Musician* interview with pianist McCoy Tyner.

[**M**cCoy Tyner] will forever be best known as the pianist in John Coltrane's famed quartet of the early 1960s, a group long since recognized as the ultimate jazz combo. ... *A Love Supreme*, recorded in 1964, is a landmark in music. ...

Tyner discusses *A Love Supreme* with us. ...

JJM: How did you meet John Coltrane?

MT: I met John in the mid 1950s. ... John came to the matinee, and I had a chance to meet him, which was a big thrill, since he was someone I really admired. His sound, his playing, his concepts. ... He was like a hero to us. ...

JJM: What special memories do you have about the recording [of *A Love Supreme*] itself? ...

MT: *A Love Supreme* was a pinnacle, where we had reached a certain point, a high point in the band in terms of communication, spiritual feelings between us. We were very good friends, and we loved playing together, and the music came first. ...

JJM: What do you remember about the day of the recording session? ...

MT: I don't think we even rehearsed that music. Usually John would play the music and then we would record it and see what could happen, because it usually developed. Once we started playing it, new ideas would form as far as interpretation of that particular song or group of songs. ...

---

landmark: *milestone*
pinnacle: *high point; top*

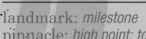

JOHN COLTRANE–PHOTO BY ESTATE OF RAEBURN FLERLAGE/MICHAEL OCHS ARCHIVES/GETTY IMAGES; BACKGROUND–SHUTTERSTOCK, ISTOCKPHOTO

Quick Fact

Coltrane became famous for his long, excited solos. Jazz critic Ira Gitler described Coltrane's technique as "sheets of sound."

Take Note

A group that changed the direction of jazz music, the Classic John Coltrane Quartet ranks #4. John Coltrane himself was a musical innovator. He was always eager to try new things. Coltrane didn't worry about keeping fans and critics happy. He hired a group of musicians who would help him explore musical boundaries.

• Coltrane broke all the rules! Although not everyone wants the rules broken, this is how music evolves and genres expand. What music do you think is breaking the rules in the 21st century? How is it breaking the rules?

The Expert Says...

"Anyone who has played modal jazz, past or present, owes a debt of gratitude to [the Classic] John Coltrane Quartet."

— Alex Henderson, allmusic.com

3 THE ROLLING

In 1986, the Rolling Stones won a Grammy Award for Lifetime Achievement. In 1994, the group won Grammys for Best Rock Album and Best Music Video.

STONES

FORMED: 1962

MUSICAL GENRE: Rock and roll

INSIDE SCOOP: In the 1960s, the Rolling Stones started saying they were the "greatest rock and roll band in the world." Forty years later it looks like they might be right!

The Stones are rock and roll royalty. But it's no coincidence that the inspiration for the band's name came from a blues song. Muddy Waters was a singer and guitarist who rose to fame playing the blues. In the 1950s, he recorded a song called "Rollin' Stone." It makes sense that a band famous for meshing rock and roll and blues into a never-before-heard musical hybrid would get its name from a blues song!

When they started out, the Rolling Stones were one of a kind. The Beatles were already becoming famous and everyone guessed that the Rolling Stones would follow their lead. People assumed they would have the same catchy sound, clean-cut look, and widespread appeal as the Beatles. But the Rolling Stones were the exact opposite! They were a dangerous alternative to the Beatles. The Stones were aggressive, rebellious, and loud!

The Rolling Stones have been making music for more than 40 years. "They are the longest-lived continuously active group in rock and roll history," according to the Rock and Roll Hall of Fame. Over the years, the group has "kept rolling, adapting to the latest sounds and styles without straying too far from their origins as a blues-loving, guitar-based rock and roll band."

hybrid: *mixture*

MUSIC MAKERS

The Rolling Stones started out performing covers of blues and soul songs. They eventually "became the breakout band of the British blues scene," writes reviewer Stephen Erlewine. As the band's fame grew, lead singer Mick Jagger and guitarist Keith Richards started writing their own material. Their first songs were an attempt at "a blues-rock fusion," according to critic Richie Unterberger.

Keith Richards, 2007

? The blues is not only a style of music. It also refers to feeling low and discouraged. What was happening politically and culturally in the 1960s that made this music meaningful? If you don't know, find out.

SINGULAR SOUND

Mick Jagger once said that his "kind of writing has always been blues-influenced because it's the music [he] grew up with." Guitarist Brian Jones also helped create the group's sound. According to Jagger, Jones "played the slide guitar at a time when no one really played it." This technique was popular among blues artists but new to rock and roll at the time. To play slide guitar, a musician puts a device called a slide over one of his or her fingers. When the slide is pressed over the strings of a guitar, it changes the pitch of the sound produced. The Stones are "the band that popularized the deepest blues," according to music critic Robert Palmer. They "went on to make something from it that was entirely their own."

? Why do you think innovative bands are often criticized? Is it because by doing something new they challenge what people think is acceptable? Explain.

Mick Jagger, 2007

ONE OF A KIND!

Originally, this band appealed to youngsters because of its dangerous new style and sound. Over the years, the Rolling Stones have proven that their longevity and popularity are one of a kind. "[N]o band since has proven to have such a broad fan base or far-reaching popularity," according to Erlewine. The Rolling Stones' influence over the last four decades has been huge. As *New York Times* music critic Kelefa Sanneh once wrote, "there is no rock 'n' roll band that doesn't owe them a debt."

Quick Fact

In 1989, the Rolling Stones were inducted into the Rock and Roll Hall of Fame. According to the museum, "No one has yet dethroned the Rolling Stones of their title as the world's greatest rock and roll band!"

The Expert Says...

" We courted adversity, took risks, and drove mothers crazy. Modeling rock in our own image we helped define the 'Rock Era.' "

— Bill Wyman, former bassist for the Rolling Stones

adversity: danger

10   9   8   7   6

ROCK ON!!

Read this list of albums to get a sense of where the Rolling Stones started out and how their music evolved over the years.

1964 THE ROLLING STONES

This album featured one song by Jagger and Richards. "Tell Me" was an acoustic-based song with a bluesy feel. Other songs were covers of works by musicians such as Chuck Berry and Buddy Holly.

1966 THE AFTERMATH

This was the first Stones album written entirely by Jagger and Richards. It "did much to define the group as the bad boys of rock and roll," according to writer Richie Unterberger.

1968 BEGGAR'S BANQUET

Beggar's Banquet "marked the return of the Rolling Stones to basic, hard-edged rock and roll," according to *Rolling Stone* magazine.

1972 EXILE ON MAIN STREET

On this album, the Stones meshed rock and roll, blues, soul, and country into one unique sound.

1981 TATTOO YOU

The single "Start Me Up" revved up interest in the band for a new decade. Music writer Stewart Mason called it "a tough little rock and roll song."

2005 A BIGGER BANG

This album "revels in the Chuck Berry boogie and classic R&B pulse that's always been [the band's] lifeblood," according to *Rolling Stone* writer Alan Light.

Quick Fact

The Rolling Stones have 10 albums on *Rolling Stone* magazine's list of the 500 Greatest Albums of All Time! Their 1972 album *Exile on Main Street* is ranked #7. "*Exile on Main Street* is the Stones at their fighting best, armed with the blues, playing to win," according to the magazine.

Take Note

The Rolling Stones roll into #3. Their rebellious style, behavior, and music have influenced generations of fans and musicians. The Rolling Stones have sold millions of albums and concert tickets worldwide.
• What current bands do you think will still be playing together 40 years from now? What elements of their music, look, and image will help them live on?

5   4   **3**   2   1

② RADIOHEAD

Radiohead has won two Grammy Awards for Best Alternative Music Album. The first was for the 1997 album OK Computer. The second was for Kid A, released in 2000.

FORMED: 1989

MUSICAL GENRE: Progressive rock

INSIDE SCOOP: Born with a paralyzed left eye, lead singer Thom Yorke had five surgeries when he was young. He turned to music to get him through this tough time.

"**R**adiohead is on a sustained run as the most interesting and innovative band in rock." Looks as if *TIME* magazine writer Josh Tyrangiel is convinced. But what is it about Radiohead that has earned the band such high praise?

Radiohead started out as a band called On A Friday. Friends Thom Yorke, Colin and Jonny Greenwood, Ed O'Brien, and Phil Selway formed this band during high school. Graduation put an end to On A Friday. But in 1991, the five friends regrouped and formed Radiohead. It didn't take long for the band to get noticed! "Creep," Radiohead's first single, was released in 1992. The song is "an intense anthem of self-loathing," according to *The Rolling Stone Encyclopedia of Rock & Roll*. Music critic Stephen Erlewine claims that the song's "angst-ridden lyrics [made] it an alternative rock anthem." The band's explosive, moody sound appealed to fans of grunge music. On later albums, Radiohead pushed its own boundaries — experimenting with electronic sounds and complicated musical arrangements. Not everyone loved these experiments. But no one could deny that the group was breaking ground on the music front.

sustained: *continuous; prolonged*
angst: *feeling of dread, anxiety, or anguish*
grunge: *style in fashion and music that originated in Seattle, characterized by moody, aggressive songs and messy clothes*

RADIOHEAD

Thom Yorke of Radiohead

MUSIC MAKERS

Thom Yorke is Radiohead's lead singer. His voice has been described as "anguished and gentle" by *Rolling Stone* magazine. Phil Selway is the band's drummer. Ed O'Brien plays guitar. Colin Greenwood is Radiohead's bassist. Jonny Greenwood, Colin's younger brother, plays guitar and keyboards. He's also been known to break out anything from a synthesizer to a xylophone for some of the band's experimental songs! Yorke's voice and Greenwood's "unconventional" playing have, according to reviewer Steve Bekkala, helped "push the boundaries of [Radiohead's] music." Bekkala also says the band has taken its music "into unusual and decidedly non-rock directions."

SINGULAR SOUND

At first, people called Radiohead a rock band. But its second album "demonstrated a growing musical scope," according to *The Rolling Stone Encyclopedia of Rock & Roll*. On *Kid A*, the band really moved beyond alternative rock. Yorke's vocals were warped with electronic sounds. The band used new instruments in experimental ways. On this album, the group combined rock, free jazz, and electronica into something entirely new.

anguished: *troubled; sorrowful*
scope: *aim; range*
electronica: *type of dance music featuring synthesizers and other electronic instruments*

ONE OF A KIND!

Each of Radiohead's albums has explored new territory. The band can't even be classified into one genre because it experiments with so many! In 2007, Radiohead did something else unique. The band's seventh album, *In Rainbows*, was first released as a digital download. Fans could only get it by downloading it from the band's Web site. The band even allowed fans to choose how much they wanted to pay for the album! And listeners weren't disappointed. As *Rolling Stone* music critic Rob Sheffield wrote, "All of [*In Rainbows*] rocks; none of it sounds like any other band on Earth."

? When bands experiment with their sound, they run the risk of alienating, or pushing away, their fans. How can bands try new things while keeping their fans happy? Is there a safe way to innovate?

Quick Fact

Radiohead has two albums on *Rolling Stone* magazine's list of the 500 Greatest Albums of All Time. Their 1995 album *The Bends* came in at #110. *OK Computer*, from 1997, ranked #162.

The Expert Says...

"The band has held on to its fans not by polishing a formula but by regularly dismantling it: each Radiohead album arrives from a new angle, with new conundrums.

— Jon Pareles, music critic for *The New York Times*

conundrums: *puzzles; mysteries*

BRITISH BAND RADIOHEAD
LETTING FANS SET THE PRICE
FOR NEW ALBUM

An article from The Canadian Press • October 1, 2007 • By Cassandra Szklarski

Long regarded as music innovators, British band Radiohead is shaking things up even more with an announcement that fans can pay as much — or as little — as they want for a digital download of [their] next album. …

Radiohead announced Monday … that fans can set their own price for a digital download of *In Rainbows*. …

Many saw the move as a snub to major record labels and the hold they have on music distribution and promotion. …

"This could be seen as a turning point in the way artists and fans interface when it comes to the release of new material," said Alan Cross, Toronto host of the syndicated radio show "The Ongoing History of New Music."

"Here is a superstar band that is out to prove that record labels are not necessary. …

interface: *interact; communicate*

"Record labels exist because of the good graces of their superstar acts. The superstar acts are the ones that pay for the operation of the label." …

Industry observer Jeremy DeBeer said the move was just the latest example of artists breaking away from major labels to gain greater control over how their music is marketed and distributed. …

"I think that what fans will appreciate most is the gesture and the creativity they're seeing from the bands that they love." …

Cross said he expected to see more such unconventional experiments.

"This is just the start. It's going to get wilder."

Quick Fact

Radiohead's video for "Just" shows a man lying down in the middle of a crowded street. Strangers pressure the man to tell them what he's doing. His secret causes everyone to lie down! Viewers dying to know what the man says are out of luck — the members of Radiohead have sworn to take the secret to their graves.

Take Note

Radiohead's innovative ways secure it the #2 spot. This band started out playing alternative rock. Since its first album, the band has been pushing the boundaries of this genre. The band members have experimented with new instruments, genres, and ways of using technology to alter their music. The recent online release of their seventh album was a first in the music industry.
• What do you think about Radiohead's method of releasing its seventh album? Do you think all music will eventually only be available on the Internet? How can record companies make people want to buy CDs?

5   4   3   **2**   1

1 THE BEATLES

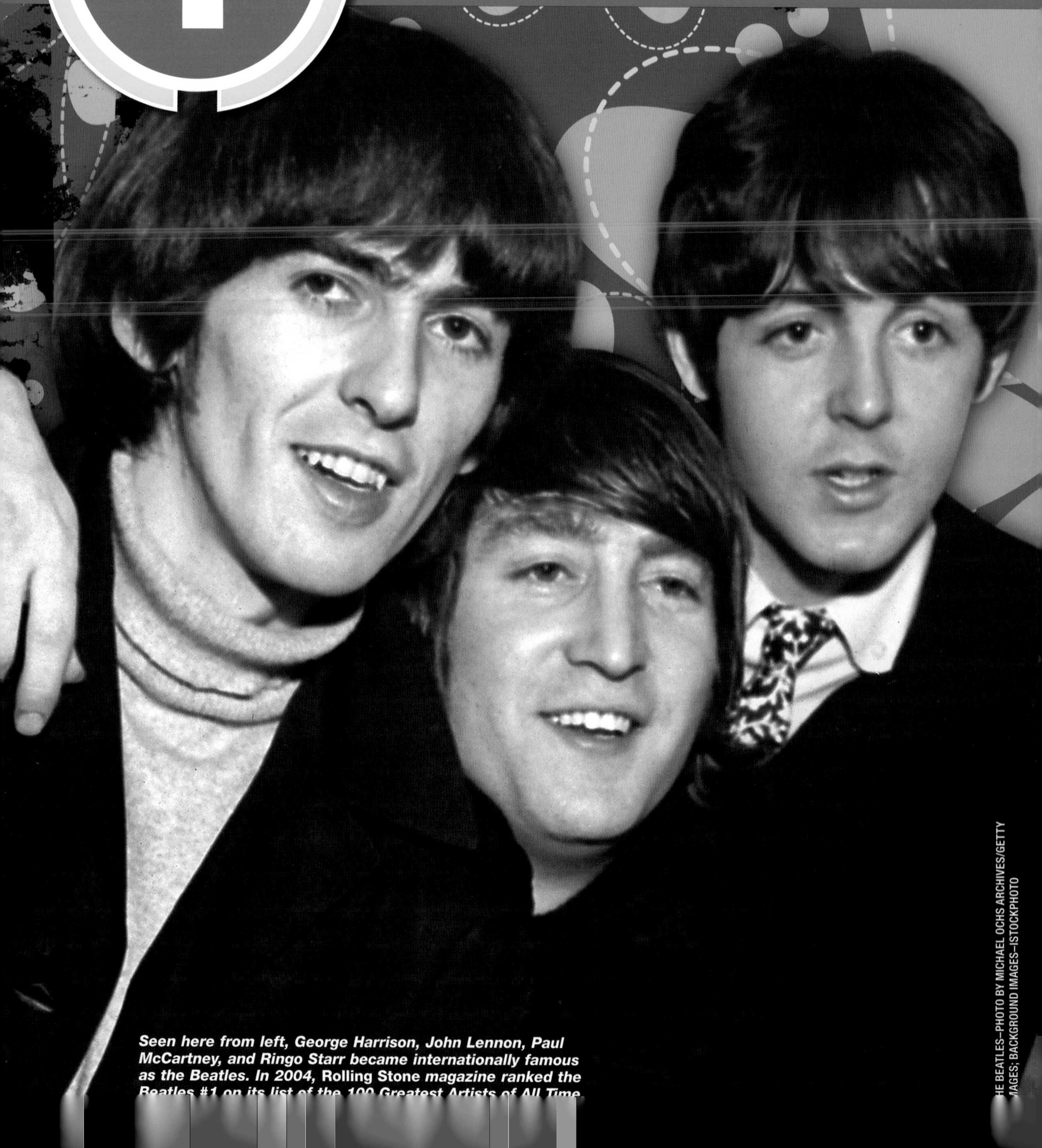

Seen here from left, George Harrison, John Lennon, Paul McCartney, and Ringo Starr became internationally famous as the Beatles. In 2004, Rolling Stone *magazine ranked the Beatles #1 on its list of the 100 Greatest Artists of All Time.*

HE BEATLES—PHOTO BY MICHAEL OCHS ARCHIVES/GETTY
MAGES; BACKGROUND IMAGES—ISTOCKPHOTO

FORMED: 1960

MUSICAL GENRE: Pop, rock and roll

INSIDE SCOOP: Despite the band's fame and huge following, the Beatles broke up only 10 years after forming their group.

The Beatles were only together for one decade. But the group accomplished things that influenced popular culture around the world! The Beatles changed everything from music and videos to literature and fashion. Their reign was short, but their impact has continued for generations.

The Beatles exploded into the worldwide music scene in 1964. This was the year the group first visited the United States. The Beatles instantly caused hysteria among fans! An appearance on *The Ed Sullivan Show* sparked a craze that came to be known as "Beatlemania." This term described the mobs of screaming fans, the new fashions, and all the Beatles merchandise the group inspired. With their "mop top" haircuts, matching suits, and catchy tunes, the Beatles also began the British Invasion of the 1960s.

If it hadn't been for the music, though, none of the other things the Beatles did would have mattered! They "synthesized all that was good about early rock and roll," according to music writer Richie Unterberger. They then "changed it into something original and even more exciting." The group's music was innovative and important. The Beatles "were the greatest and most influential act of the rock era," according to Unterberger. "They introduced more innovations into popular music than any other rock band of the 20th century."

THE BEATLES

MUSIC MAKERS

The members of this group originally went by the name The Quarrymen. They later changed their name to Johnny and the Moondogs and then to the Silver Beetles. In 1960, they settled on a name that would soon be famous — the Beatles. At first, the group played at small clubs in Liverpool, England. Once they started becoming famous, people nicknamed them the "Fab Four." At this time, the group consisted of John Lennon, Paul McCartney, George Harrison, and Ringo Starr. Lennon and McCartney wrote most of the band's songs.

? During the 1960s, the Beatles starred in movies such as *A Hard Day's Night*. These movies are considered an early type of music video. How might these movies have influenced the Beatles' popularity? How might they have affected music videos in the future?

The Expert Says...

" Before the Beatles ... you didn't have rockers deliberately putting things out of balance. ... You can't exaggerate the license that this gave to everyone from Motown to Jimi Hendrix. "

— Elvis Costello, musician

? By challenging traditions and trying new things, the Beatles "put things out of balance," according to Elvis Costello. How might this have paved the way for other musicians?

SINGULAR SOUND

In the early years, the Beatles wrote infectious, catchy melodies. Their music borrowed traditional elements from rock and roll and rhythm and blues. Later on, the group experimented with everything from folk and gospel to psychedelic rock. They also played instruments from other cultures, such as the sitar, on several songs. In 1966, the Beatles released *Revolver*. Many songs on the album featured orchestral arrangements. The group recorded with violins, cellos, and other string instruments. Many Beatles songs were also recognizable thanks to the group's use of brass instruments such as trumpets and horns. The use of so many different instruments helped the Beatles create an innovative, unique rock sound. The group's next album, *Sgt. Pepper's Lonely Hearts Club Band*, was "rock's ultimate declaration of change," according to *Rolling Stone* magazine.

ONE OF A KIND!

The Beatles launched the "British Invasion that made rock truly an international phenomenon," according to writer Richie Unterberger. The group's fame was one of a kind. Their impact has never been repeated. The Beatles broke up more than 35 years ago. However, the group's music continues to be hugely popular. "[N]o group has so radically transformed the sound and significance of rock and roll," according to *The Rolling Stone Encyclopedia of Rock & Roll*.

psychedelic rock: *music with a bizarre, unusual sound, confusing or nonsensical lyrics, and a dreamy feel*
sitar: *stringed instrument from India*

Quick Fact

The Beatles were one of the first groups to record with a Mellotron. A Mellotron is a type of synthesizer that allows samples to be prerecorded and then played back. The group used the innovative instrument on "Strawberry Fields Forever."

8   7   6

Here, There and Everywhere!

The Beatles helped to popularize rock and roll around the world. They also helped the genre evolve into a true art form. Learn more about the group's fame in this list of Fab Four facts.

The Beatles had 11 albums on *Rolling Stone* magazine's list of the 500 Greatest Albums of All Time — *Sgt. Pepper's Lonely Hearts Club Band* was #1! This innovative album "is simply the best of everything the Beatles ever did as musicians, pioneers, and pop stars, all in one place," according to the magazine.

"Yesterday," from the group's 1965 album *Help!,* is the most frequently-covered Beatles song. One of the most famous covers is a 1967 soul version by Ray Charles.

In 1967, the Beatles made TV history. The group performed "All You Need is Love" on live TV. The performance was part of the first TV show ever broadcast live around the world! More than 350 million people tuned in.

The Beatles 1 was released in 2000. This album featured every one of the Beatles' #1 hit singles released between 1962 and 1970 — 27 in all! At the time of its release, *The Beatles 1* became the fastest-selling album ever. It also reached #1 on the Billboard charts.

Twenty-three of the group's songs made it onto *Rolling Stone* magazine's list of the 500 Greatest Songs of All Time.

Take Note

The Beatles easily take the #1 spot! This band sparked the British Invasion of the 1960s. This helped to popularize rock and roll. It also paved the way for other international groups. The Beatles experimented with genre, technique, technology, and sound. In the process, the group opened doors for other musical innovators.
• What Beatles influences do you notice in popular music today? Which bands have acknowledged learning something from the Beatles? If you don't know, find out.

Quick Fact

At one point in 1964, the Beatles held the top five spots on the Billboard Hot 100 chart! "Can't Buy Me Love" was #1, "Twist and Shout" was #2, "She Loves Me" was #3, "I Want to Hold Your Hand" was #4, and "Please Please Me" was #5.

5   4   3   2   1

We Thought ...

Here are the criteria we used in ranking the 10 most innovative bands.

The band:
- Changed the direction of music
- Inspired technological changes in the music industry
- Influenced other musicians
- Changed what people listened to
- Was groundbreaking
- Is critically acclaimed
- Has had lasting fame
- Influenced pop culture
- Introduced ancient musical traditions to worldwide audiences
- Blended genres to create something new

What Do You Think?

1. Do you agree with our ranking? If you don't, try ranking these bands yourself. Justify your ranking with data from your own research and reasoning. You may refer to our criteria, or you may want to draw up your own list of criteria.

2. Here are three other innovative bands that we considered but in the end did not include on our top 10 list: Grupo Fantasma, Pink Floyd, and Wu-Tang Clan.
   - Find out more about these bands. Do you think they should have made our list? Give reasons for your response.
   - Are there other innovative bands that you think should have made our list? Explain your choices.

Index